HONOLULU

THEN & NOW

By ROLAND MORGAN

CITY AND COUNTY OF HONOLULU · STATE OF HAWAII

Bodima Books

ISBN-0-88875 - 003-X

Cover design by Roland Morgan and Bob Masse; artwork by Bob Masse

This book is for Dilys and Tudor

**Honolulu's
Hawaiian Directions**

Mauka
(towards the mountains)
Ewa
(towards Pearl Harbor)
Waikiki
(towards Diamond Head)
Makai
(towards the sea)

A Bodima Book

13 Estates Drive, Orinda, California 94563

Introduction

A collection of flashbacks puts the present next to the past and raises some questions about both. But throughout there is the emergent question of the third comparative photograph, the missing future. Will decentralization shrink the towering skylines? Will architecture learn to live with climate again, instead of refrigerating it away? Will the driver evolve into a walker, a runner and a rider? How will solar energy and the planned economy change the look of a tropical city? Will the country infiltrate the town? This collection of comparative photographs shows the process of urban growth. At the same time it shows how rapidly the set of the movie we live in changes. There is no reason to believe it cannot rapidly change direction according to economic and social influences.

The transformation of Honolulu can thus be extrapolated to include factors more or less random, according to the way you look at them, like oil rationing and drought, or it can be projected according to the obvious growth trend in the area covered and the catch-up futures of the hinterland—will the Kona coast go high-rise? Will Maui become a suburban Oahu?

In some ways a balanced future will mean rediscovering the past, and the sheer speed of 20th century development invites nostalgia for the Waikiki of Victorian adventure, the organic horse-drawn environment, the quietness, the darkness.

But behind the picturesque was the grotesque: venereal disease, leprosy, plague, tuberculosis, extermination of sandalwood and whale, illiteracy, to name only a few afflictions. The native culture now embalmed for tourism was so despotic, sexist and superstitious that the female half of the Hawaiian race abandoned it at the first opportunity. As for the beloved horse, even if oil ran out tomorrow, drivers would use booze, sewage, sunshine, hot air, anything, to keep their cars running.

The set may never be picturesque again. The mess we live with is the result of so many conveniences. When students of urban affairs come to use comparative photography in the history of human habitat they will find that ugliness does not denote a bad living environment any more thanpicturesqueness indicates the garden of Eden. Many modern buildings are inside out. External appearances are sacrificed, even exaggerated, for a functional interior. Old buildings were the opposite. Absurd sacrifices were made to have a bank look like a Doric temple, or a barracks like a feudal fortress. We may settle for isolated sanctuaries, memory lanes where old urban sets are preserved.

American cities are poised near the end of the phase of central growth, towards the top of an exponential curve. Far from proceeding by lazy 'Hawaiian time' Hawaii is mutating into the future as fast as anywhere in the U.S.A. Suburban clones are sprouting everywhere, forcing legislators to question the ultimate carrying capacity of the state. The more it grows, the more it relies on imports factored by the big landowners. As it grows, the landowners' estates multiply in value. Even if the big estates accepted that limits on growth would immediately boost the value of development areas it is hard to see who could preside over such an apportionment in a market economy.

At the same time at points around the globe Hawaii is being touted as a tropical paradise draped with airbrushed hula girls. Tourists are invited to get away from it all in a city of hotels which by 1990 might house 200,000 (at double occupancy). Here the growth is doubly problematic. Tourism is the state's biggest industry, and a successful industry is axiomatically a growing one. Yet growth in this industry threatens the very product that is being sold: the environment. Inviting people over compounds the problem because so many want to come back to stay and 'me last' is an unconstitutional cry that confounds any politician who tries to exploit it. So, in the dilemma of the age, the unlimitable has to go on a diet. Some of the recipes have been pinned on the kitchen wall. A subway route is drawn up, a ferry system has been studied, surveys of historic buildings have been made, growth targets set,

decentralization adopted solar power publicized. But as yet the only decisive action is at Pearl Harbor where the U.S. navy, with military logic, has a fleet of free bicycles.

******

The comparative layouts jump about geographically to give a fresh, kaleidoscopic look at the process of change. They generally repeat a sequence of view, street scene, building.

References to history in the captions only briefly sketch the dramatic story of Honolulu, which is thoroughly covered in the extensive bibliography of Hawaiiana. The most accessible is Feher's **Pictorial History of Hawaii**. Few escape the pervasive influence of tourist mythology.

Grateful acknowledgment goes to Agnes Conrad and the staff at Hawaii state archives; Deborah Sullivan and the staff at the Bishop Museum; Frances Jackson at the University of Hawaii archives; the staff at Photoplant; Dr. Otto Degener; Joe Mullins; all the people who opened doors along the path of the old photographers; and not forgetting the intrepid photographers themselves.

Roland Morgan
Mokuleia Beach
O'ahu

Index

BM denotes Bishop Museum, UH University of Hawaii, SA State Archives. All photographs by permission.

THEN Honolulu makai panorama 1885

Kou, Hawaii's only natural harbor, is the historic focus of Honolulu's growth dating back to its discovery by an English captain in 1792. A century later, when U.S. forces arrived during the Phillipines campaign, Pearl Harbor (out of picture, right) was developed and industry moved in that direction. Honolulu is a translation of Fair Haven, the short-lived English name for the harbor.

1

NOW Honolulu makai panorama

Building on a modern scale, including the drainage system, came with Hawaii's annexation into the U.S.A. during the Spanish-American war. Honolulu's cosmopolitan architecture today matches any comparable mainland city's. One peculiarity is the preponderance of offices downtown, most shopping having moved to the big Ala Moana center (out of picture left) in the early 1960's. The 1968 state capitol (left of center) stands out appropriately in this Punchbowl view.

THEN **King and Alakea Streets ewa makai 1883**
   Billboards were banned in the islands in the 1920's. These early examples show Waikiki beach accommodation at $12 a week and Bull Durham, the first world-wide smoking campaign. The old telegraph pole (left) has been superseded by a tall new telephone pole for the service introduced to Honolulu in 1880.

3

NOW King and Alakea Streets ewa makai
This site is now occupied by the 1960's Finance Factors
building, which features a unique array of adjustable louvered
windows relying on electric light—a rejection of the climate.

THEN **Fort and Queen Streets makai 1950**

The powerful Hackfeld company had too many Hamburg connections for it to survive seizure during the 1914-18 European war, when it was renamed American Factors, later Amfac. The company's characterful 1901 stone pile boasted an ornate interior of marble, mosaic, wrought iron, fine wood and frescoes; certainly a unique Honolulu interior.

NOW **Fort and Queen Streets makai**
In 1968 American Factors tore down the
Hackfeld building to replace it with one of
their soaring 20-story foreshore towers.

THEN Honolulu ewa panorama 1895

The royal seat of power photographed a few years after the republican take-over. At left the Aliiolani Hale, at right the Iolani Palace. Office blocks and towers, shooting up in San Francisco, were yet to arrive at the crossroads of the Pacific.

NOW Honolulu ewa panorama

Honolulu's government center remains intact while the downtown core is transformed by a hodge-podge of office towers of varying degrees of obsolescence. In the foreground are the gardens of the Kawaiaha'o church where the picture is taken from. About half the land area in the picture is under occupation by motor vehicles, including the multi-storied parkade (mid-right), much larger than the trust company tower on its left.

THEN **Hotel Street at King waikiki 1898** (left)
The lei-makers (right) convey the intimate feel of the old harbor town shopping district. A boy could wander down the center of his street. Davey the photographer took some of the pictures in this book.

NOW **Hotel Street at King waikiki**
Development of the world's biggest shopping center two miles away at the gates of Waikiki's hotel stronghold froze this old focal point into the 1950's. Solar-powered overhead transit would bring a swift transformation.

THEN 250 South Hotel 1895

Spacious oval lanais were added to the front of the original Royal Hawaiian Hotel at the peak of its career as Honolulu's social center. Within a few years of this photo however, the nearby Young Hotel and the Moana and Seaside on Waikiki had taken most of the business and in 1917 the Royal Hawaiian was converted to a Young Men's Christian Association hostel.

NOW 250 South Hotel

The new YMCA building was opened in 1928, its two front lanais echoing the design of the old hotel.

THEN **Looking west on**
Nuuanu Pali pass 1885
    This rugged road led from the
busy port of Honolulu to the
tranquil Hawaiian farmlands of
Kaneohe. Here modern Hawaii's
founder, King Kamehameha,
defeated the warlord of O'ahu in
1795 using guns obtained from
foreign traders.

NOW looking west on Nuuanu Pali pass

In the 1920's a smoother route was blasted between the peaks, but in the post-war boom this road became jammed and today's tunnels were drilled through the rock a hundred feet below.

THEN Kaneohe panorama north 1878

Primitive sugar mills like the one (center) at the foot of Lilipuna Road did not last long against the technology of cane kings like Claus Spreckels, who was at this time financing the Hawaiian government. Much of the area was still farmed by Hawaiians and Chinese. Fishponds (upper right) supplied the tables of Hawaiian chiefs. Typifying Hawaii's concentrated land ownership, sugar baron James Castle bought 340,000 acres here in 1917.

NOW **Kaneohe panorama north**
The arrival of suburban Honolulu
has driven housing prices out of many
people's reach. Isolated pockets of
surviving farmers fight to keep their
land.

THEN Ewa on King Street at Fort 1885

Honolulu's **haole's** built a harbor town just like on the mainland. Such was the quietness of downtown Honolulu in 1885 that just about all the folks knew they were having their picture taken. Night-time street lighting would not be introduced until the end of the decade.

NOW Ewa on King Street at Fort
Strangely devoid of shopping and, even more strangely, of a hotel, downtown Honolulu's one-way traffic arteries are no longer impressed by having their picture taken—a shutterbug could get run down, even if by a $20,000 sports model.

THEN **Fort Street at Pauahi waikiki makai 1890**
    The catholic cathedral of Honolulu opened in 1843, after a decade of missionary
opposition was overruled. Iron railings enclosed a spacious meeting yard.

NOW **Fort Street at Pauahi waikiki makai**
Modified extensively over the years, the cathedral gained weighty Doric pillars
in 1929. With later removal of traffic from Fort Street the yard went open plan.

THEN **Manoa Valley ewa panorama 1920**
   Hawaii Hall (center) was the first building on the Hawaii College 90-acre campus in 1912. This scene shows the college after it was named University of Hawaii, engineering quad at left, university farm in the foreground.

NOW **Manoa Valley ewa panorama**
   Hale Manoa tower in the foreground demonstrates the dynamic growth of the university population. To its right is the Kennedy Theatre. Hawaii Hall is dwarfed amidst the 50 or so buildings added to campus. In the distance is the dense housing area towards Punchbowl.

THEN Chinatown 1886
The upper veranda frame building favored by the Chinese provided open air space for urban dwellers, most of them with businesses downstairs, and shade for the sidewalk beneath. Few examples of this once typical Hawaiian architecture survive.

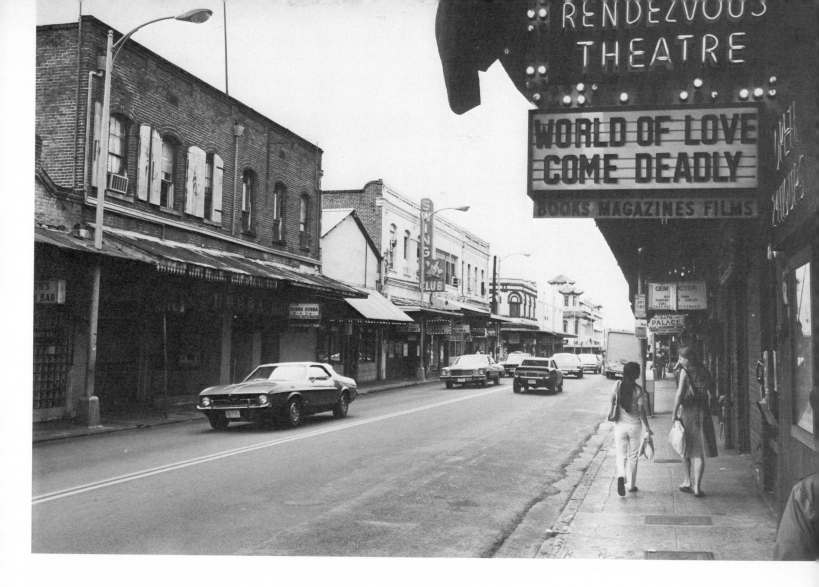

NOW Chinatown

While much of Hotel Street's commercial architecture dates back to the turn of the century its confusion of styles and the nature of local business suggest that even if Honolulu's planned rail transit relieves Hotel Street of its congestion, many buildings will be replaced. An urban renewal program also promises to raze most of the district.

THEN 841 Bishop 1950 (left)

The Theo. H. Davies building was built in 1919 for one of Hawaii's 'big five' trading companies, from an otherwise forgotten downtown plan drawn up by its architect. A striking Italian Renaissance design made entirely from reinforced concrete and cut stone, the building doubled as offices and warehouse, incorporating loading bays at the rear.

NOW 841 Bishop

Tragically the warehousing function of the Davis building became incompatible with downtown Honolulu in the 1970's and the high-rise Davies Pacific Center was built in its place. Imaginative street level design, however, gave the city a new space which made up for the architectural loss.

THEN **mauka panorama from judiciary building 1891** (left)
At right is the barracks of the royal guard. At center is Iolani Palace, occupied by the ill-fated Queen Liliuokalani. At left behind the palace is the royal private quarters, beyond it in the distance are St. Andrew's Cathedral and the Royal Hawaiian Hotel. Railings had been substituted for the high palace walls by a jittery legislature in 1890. Coats of arms on the gates show the monarchy still intact.

NOW **mauka panorama from judiciary building**
The 1968 legislature occupies the site of the barracks which in turn occupy the site of the royal bungalow. After serving as the republican executive building for 75 years the restored palace was opened to the public exactly a century after its founding.

THEN Fort Street at Hotel makai 1898
Honolulu's main shopping street in the heyday of the modern city. Most of the conveniences, few of the blights. Windows were shuttered in case of riots in the streets. The electric arc lamp (bottom right) was on a pulley for daily replacement of the arc.

NOW Fort Street at Hotel makai
The aging commercial structures of Fort Street,
overshadowed by business towers, invite redevelopment.

THEN Kapiolani Park 1900
No North American town in the horse-drawn age could imagine life without somewhere to race the steeds and place some bets on the results. The long-forgotten structures of the Kapiolani Park race track looked ghostly without their crowds.

NOW Kapiolani Park

Where gaitered puritans and barefoot immigrants once mingled for a horse race their descendants gather at 7 a.m. on a Sunday morning for a bracing run. Diamond Head looms unmoved.

THEN **Honolulu waikiki panorama 1887**
    The old New England missionary church of 1842, Kawaiaha'o, became the shrine of Hawaiian royalty. King Lunalilo had his tomb built by the church door in 1874. Beyond stretch the swamps of Ala Moana, Kewalo Basin and Ala Wai, Diamond Head swathed in haze.

NOW Honolulu waikiki panorama
The architecturally undistinguished territorial building was built in 1926 to house government offices. It is shown here under restoration. Diamond Head is lost behind a wall of towers at Waikiki.

THEN Fort Street mauka view 1859

A new landmark on Fort Street was the Congregational church (spire, center) built by the missionaries for Honolulu's **haole** population in 1852. The Bartlett Saloon (bottom left) would have been out of bounds for Hawaiian natives. At far left are the offices of pioneer photographer J.L. Chase, who took the picture.

35

N OW Fort street mauka view

After a period of intense traffic congestion, some of the greenery has returned to Fort Street. The commercial buildings date back to the turn of the century, disguised by numerous facelifts. Most shopping has moved away from old Honolulu to new shopping centers.

THEN 140 South King Street 1925
The Bank of Hawaii moved from its Merchant Street premises in the 1920's to a building in the Mediterranan style favored by members of the 'big five' trading companies in the same era, giving downtown Honolulu a period of pleasing architectural consistency in tune with the climate.

NOW 140 South King Street

By the 1960's the high-rise opportunities were too tempting and the bank moved across King Street to the Castle and Cooke financial plaza. The bank building was demolished and replaced by the sheer International-style tower of the Bishop Trust, handsomely sheathed in sepia-tinted reflecting glass.

THEN Waikiki Beach 1880
The Occidental Hotel (left) was owned by a steamship line. The royal villa was a few yards further down the beach. A sober suit, beard and hat were the **haole** uniform.

NOW Waikiki Beach(right)
Jet planes bring millions of sun-seekers to Waikiki every year and the set is transformed, but the underlying pattern remains the same, with many of the hotels interlinked by ownership with their carriers. **Haole's** stripped to loin cloths in the 1920's in search of the tan made fashionable by the jazz age.

THEN **Hobron Lane at Ala Moana makai 1944**
It's not far back in time to a Waikiki of sandy lanes, ramshackle beach huts and happy-go-lucky parking.

41

NOW **Hobron Lane at Ala Moana makai**
Honolulu's big yacht marina was built at the foot of Hobron Lane soon after installation of Ala Moana boulevard in 1954. Accommodation racks servicing jet age tourists now crowd the beach and cars stop on the streets only in the small hours.

THEN Kailua 1920

A former captial of O'ahu, Kailua once held the bulk of the island's Hawaiian population. They lived among cocoanut groves and fishponds which have since turned into inland swamps. By 1920 a metalled coast road had been installed and Honolulu's suburbs were moving in.

NOW Kailua

Kailua is now a model grid suburb, connected to Honolulu by two freeways through the mountains.

THEN Honolulu waterfront 1895
Trade was concentrated within three blocks either side of Fort Street, light offshore schooners mooring agaist international clippers willy-nilly. Giant wooden vessels (right) were being replaced by ships with iron hulls.

NOW Honolulu waterfront

The Glasgow-built Falls Of Clyde, one of the last iron-hulled sailors to pass through Honolulu, is now moored permanently where there once was a forest of masts. At her side is a typical train from the narrow guage Oahu Railway and Land Company line which founded the Dillingham empire.

THEN Bishop and Queen Streets mauka ewa 1915
Institutional solidarity was the aim of the Ionic pillared classical facade. Sugar factors Castle and Cooke, one of Hawaii's 'big five' oligarchs, occupied these grand premises for the first half of the 20th century.

NOW Bishop and Queen Streets mauka ewa (right)
The company's 1968 building, the Financial Plaza of the Pacific, employed the 'brutalist' style, commonly known as waffle-iron, again suggesting sobriety and institutional solidarity.

THEN **Honolulu mauka panorama 1894**
From the top of the Iolani Palace the Hawaiian monarchs had a reassuring view of the nearby barracks of the royal guard, a toy Crusader fortress built in 1870. The stables and armory are at left. Beyond, hidden in the trees is Washington Place. Note the windmill at center, an economical well water pump on the breezy punchbowl slope.

49

NOW **Honolulu mauka panorama**
The 1968 state capital cost $25 million. Surrounded by water, like the islands, its forty columns recall palm trees and the roof evokes the nearby volcanic creaters. The fortress barracks were removed stone by stone to the Iolani Palace grounds for a museum.

THEN Fort Street at King mauka 1910

The 1902 cigar store at left and the 1900 bank building at right both flaunt the fashionable 'Sullivanesque' carved decor, and flourish candy-stripe awnings which served both to brighten up the street and attract business while offering shade. The streetcar was an energy-efficient, non-polluting form of fairly rapid transit. At left towers the Hackfeld store, later Liberty House.

NOW Fort Street at King mauka
Vehicle traffic on Fort Street at peak times became ridiculous (inset 1950's) and Honolulu joined the 1960's trend towards downtown pedestrian zones, although many wish the concept could have been more widely applied. Beneath King Street is an imaginative subway walk with ornamental lagoon.

THEN 2200 Kalakaua Avenue 1930
This elegant branch of a San Francisco curio dealer opened soon after the Royal Hawaiian Hotel on Waikiki beach, catering to Waikiki's steamship set. It boasted the latest in chic, including carpeted walls.

53

NOW 2200 Kalakaua Avenue

Gumps could not make a go of it on Waikiki's main street as the clientele changed and the 'architectural gem' built for the store now houses airline offices and a hamburger outlet, unnoticed by tourists in the shadow of the Bank of Hawaii tower.

THEN **Sans Souci beach 1890** (left)
The San Souci (Carefree) hotel was the leading guest house in the 1890's, before Honolulu's business establishment built the four-story Moana hotel. An observation tower offered a lookout point for landmarks.

NOW **San Souci beach**
Apartment and hotel towers sprang up along the beach in the 1960's, the quality of the design falling far short of the value of the real estate.

THEN **Nuuanu stream from King Street 1890**
 Chinatown was the main victim of an outbreak of bubonic plague
among inadequately quarantined immigrants. In 1900 a fire was set
which spread through the district, destroying the Kaumakapili church
which for years had served as the community center. In this era of poor
drainage the stream was an open sewer.

NOW **Nuuanu stream from King Street**
Giant apartment towers demonstrate the 25-fold
increase in Honolulu's population. Consolidation of Aala
Park (left) narrowed the stream's flow in 1900.

THEN Merchant and Fort Streets waikiki makai 1913
  These early Honolulu office buildings are (left) the 1901 Stangenwald building, briefly the city's tallest, and the 1894 Judd building, housing at this time the Bank of Hawaii, which moved out in 1927. The Ionic columns in the doorway were a banking necessity.

NOW **Merchant and Fort Streets waikiki makai**
Encumbered with added stories, these two typical Victorians have survived the downtown boom and lend character to historic Merchant Street.

THEN **Diamond Head from Punchbowl 1890**
In the foreground beyond the parapet is the comfortable residential area spreading out around King Street. Beyond are the marshes and ponds behind Waikiki. At left are some of the rice and taro fields which fed the fast-growing immigrant population. Since O'ahu's building boom began in the 1950's, land speculation has eliminated productive small-holdings such as these, most foodstuffs being imported.

NOW Diamond Head from Punchbowl

Drainage of the Waikiki district by the Ala Wai canal in the 1920's opened the area up for development, which was leisurely until the phenomenal growth of jet age tourism by 1978 had deposited three million visitors a year in Waikiki's accommodation racks. At far right is the tower of the Ala Moana center (1959-65) with which the Dillingham corporation put most of Honolulu's retailing under one roof.

THEN Kalakaua Avenue at Kapahulu 1865

Laced with streams and ponds, Waikiki was always a more pleasant place than hot, dusty Honolulu, which existed solely for its port. The wealthy maintained beach villas, while farmers grew rice and taro inland. Exactly why people raced along Kalakaua, as the sign seems to indicate, is open to conjecture. It reads: Driving faster than a walk across this bridge will be prosecuted according to law

NOW Kalakaua Avenue at Kapahulu

A century later the world has discovered Waikiki, with millions visiting every year. This spot is one of the few that still offer a view of Diamond Head.

THEN **Queen Street at Fort waikiki makai 1875**
Originally built as Honolulu courthouse in 1852, this
classically simple building later housed the royal
Hawaiian legislature. After a feud between royal factions
in 1874 the legislature was removed to the new Aliiolane
Hale and the courthouse was sold to Hackfeld and Co.,
one of the Hawaiian 'big five' trading companies.

65

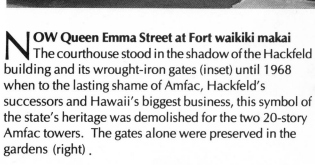

NOW **Queen Emma Street at Fort waikiki makai**
The courthouse stood in the shadow of the Hackfeld
building and its wrought-iron gates (inset) until 1968
when to the lasting shame of Amfac, Hackfeld's
successors and Hawaii's biggest business, this symbol of
the state's heritage was demolished for the two 20-story
Amfac towers. The gates alone were preserved in the
gardens (right) .

THEN **Pearl Harbor mauka view 1941** (left)

The Sunday morning attack on O'ahu by 360 Japanese warplanes led to the U.S.A.'s nuclear attack on Japan four years later. Six ships were sunk and twelve others crippled in a few minutes of bombardment.

NOW **Pearl Harbor mauka VIEW** (right)

U.S.N. warships are deployed all over the Pacific, seen in Pearl Harbor mostly for refits. The navy has another fleet to handle harbor congestion: hundreds of free bicycles are issued to workers here (but not downtown).

THEN **Union and Hotel Streets ewa mauka 1914**
    Flower sellers brightened the sidewalks of less congested streets. Within a few years the streetcar
and horse and carriage would succumb to motor vehicles.

NOW Union and Hotel Streets ewa mauka
With Union Street closed to vehicles, narrow Hotel Street carries the bulk of Honolulu's downtown bus traffic. Riders wait where flower sellers once sat.

70

THEN **2365 Kalakaua Avenue ewa makai 1920**
   The center building of Waikiki's original grand hotel, the Moana, was built in 1901. The wings were added in 1918, fitted with different woods on each floor.

NOW 2365 Kalakaua Avenue ewa makai
In 1977 the Moana had a million-dollar refit, restoring the spacious Palm Court elegance of the
steamship era. Parvenue accommodation racks now crowd around the Edwardian dowager.

THEN **Honolulu harbor mauka panorama 1890**
  Bounded by the towers of Kaumakapili church (left) and Kawaiaha'o (right), the Honolulu waterfront was dwarfed by the masts of local traders (left), international merchants (center) and the more or less obsolete masts of a steamer (right). A posed Hawaiian recalls a traditional fishing technique.

NOW Honolulu harbor mauka panorama

The 1926 Aloha Tower, which houses a 160-foot high shipping control room, came to symbolize Hawaii's passenger steamship era. Honolulu's own Oceanic and Matson lines moored at its foot, as did dozens of international visitors before the jet age. Sand Island in the foreground has been transformed by dredging fill. Under construction behind the smokestacks of the oil-burning electric company is the 30-story Grosvenor tower.

THEN **Fort Street at Merchant mauka 1908** (left)
  The popularity of bicycles at the turn of the century made city streets a convivial environment. As now, architects made few concessions to the Hawaiian climate. On Fort Street trimmed canopies shaded the sidewalk from noon hour sun, but otherwise the two and three-story corniced commercial buildings could have been in London or Philadelphia.

75

NOW Fort Street at Merchant mauka

Two savings bank towers now soar above a Fort Street closed to vehicle traffic. At left the 1977 Pioneer Plaza incorporates canopy slabs over tinted windows which are kept closed to seal in electronically cooled air. Thus vast energy expenses bring what was formerly achieved by breezes and paperweights.

THEN **1018 Lunalilo Street 1899** (left)
Honolulu's leading owners had luxurious homes on the slopes of the punchbowl. From under the bough of a koa tree this splendid garden looked towards Tantalus ridge.

NOW **1018 Lunalilo Street**
Growth of urban population from 39,000 in 1900 to about 700,000 in 1978 has meant the transformation of areas like the Punchbowl slopes to dense housing, mostly in apartment racks like this one, which occupied the site in 1970.

T **HEN Honolulu mauka panorama 1950** (left)

An Edwardian roof garden topped the 195-room Alexander Young hotel for 40 years. Construction of the block-long building in 1903 marked the arrival of modern-scale architecture in Honolulu. At left are the arched windows of the Portland building at Union Street. Beyond is the spire, later removed, of Our Lady Of Peace cathedral.

N **OW Honolulu mauka panorama**

New owners put offices on the roof of the Young Hotel as it lost business to Waikiki. At left the Portland building survives opposite the 1940 Kress store.

THEN Waimanolo 1881

Sugar planter John Cummins had 600 acres under cane with his own railway serving a wharf. Formerly Waimanolo's fertile plain had been Hawaiian farming country and the site of a temple. Few Hawaiians worked the cane, leaving it to immigrant labor.

N OW Waimanolo
This big tract of land is now occupied by the
obsolescent Bellows air force base, one of O'ahu's many
examples of controversial federal government
ownership.

THEN **Waialua Bay 1900** (left)
The railway age produced the resort hotel. O'ahu's excellent example was the Haleiwa hotel, built by the Dillingham railway on its narrow guage line from Honolulu to Kahuku. Generously fitted with double verandas, or **lanais**, and featuring an amusing footbridge of woven branches in the garden, the hotel boasted an interior entirely fitted in **koa**, Hawaii's beautiful cabinet wood, now a rarity (right).

NOW **Waialua Bay** (left)
The old hotel succumbed to the ravages of termites. An officers' mess in World War II, it finally closed with the railway soon after the war and was replaced by a local tavern. Alterations for Haleiwa's marina have changed the waterfront.

THEN **Nuuanu Valley mauka 1853**
This early daguerrotype shows the comfortable homesteads of Honolulu's foreign merchant population, at this time enjoying the prosperity caused by the California gold rush. Other early photographs show that the whole city looked like this—comfortable lots from coast to mountains.

NOW **Nuuanu Valley mauka**
The valley's residential character remains unchanged, bar some increase in density. From early days, Honolulu residents sought the cooler air of higher slopes, but only in the motor age would they settle on Pacific (right) or Kapalama (left) heights.

THEN **Merchant Street at Kaahumanu mauka waikiki 1884**
The 1881 Hawaiian Gazette building saw the semiofficial
Gazette combine with the **Pacific Commercial Advertizer**, a
merger which eventually produced the Honolulu **Advertizer**.

NOW Merchant Street at Kaahumanu makiki waikiki
The historic Gazette building, unprotected by heritage
designation, was demolished to make way for the 1977 Pioneer
Plaza tower.

THEN **Queen Street at Fort waikiki 1881**
    This pre-telephone picture shows the typical Victorian commercial structures that serviced Honolulu's busy harbor. A modern-scale four-story structure would not appear for two decades.

NOW Queen Street at Fort waikiki

Today the same area is completely high-rise, with Queen Street a one-way canyon. An exception, many wonder for how long, is the C. Brewer building, head office of one of Hawaii's 'big five' trading companies, the gardens of which can be seen at left.

THEN 1302 Queen Emma Street 1885 (left)

Keeping up royal appearances princess Ruth Keelikolani, last grandchild of Kamehameha I, matched the newly-built Iolani Palace with her own Nob Hill home nearby. The corpulent chieftess occupied her Second Empire extravaganza for only a few weeks before she died. The dream home was sold to banker C.R. Bishop.

NOW 1302 Queen Emma Street

The house ended its days as a grammar school and in 1926 it was razed to make way for the classically decorated central intermediate school.

THEN Honolulu makai panorama 1887 (left)
Iolani Palace had a clear view across the tree-shaded town to Honolulu harbor's tall ships. The French Second Empire-style corner tower displays the thoroughness of Victorian builders.

NOW Honolulu makai panorama (above)
As soon as they took over the state Hawaii's businessmen set about building the downtown business core. The 30-story Grosvenor Center tower under construction on the waterfront will keep Honolulu in the architectural big league, but such edifices may be rendered obsolete before the end of the century.

THEN **Foot of Nuuanu Street mauka 1877**
  Honolulu was founded for its harbor and throughout the 19th century its major business buildings were
the warehouses of the waterfront. At right the bowsprit of a wooden cargo vessel.

NOW Foot of Nuuanu Street mauka
Some turn of the century buildings survive near the foot of Nuuanu. Voyages of the facsimile Polynesian yacht **Hokule'a** (in the foreground) have symbolized Hawaii's continuing study of its cultural heritage.

THEN **Beretania at Richards Street mauka 1891**
   Plans for a Church of England cathedral were laid in 1861, during a period of British influence. A cornerstone laid in 1867 languished for 17 years until cut stone for the arches, columns and windows was brought from England. The chancel seen here was finished by 1896, although the cathedral was not complete until 1901, 40 years after conception.

NOW **Beretania at Richards Street mauka** (right)
   The front of St. Andrew's was extended in 1958 to incorporate a stained glass wall.

THEN Lanikai Beach 1923

This picture shows Honolulu's suburbs creeping along the Windward coast of O'ahu the way suburbs are now spreading in the outer islands half a century later. In the distance, towards Alala Point, the subdivisions are filling up, while at Lanikai Beach only a couple of houses have been completed.

NOW Lanikai Beach
The Windward beaches and plains now carry a population of over 100,000.

THEN King Street waikiki from Fort 1895 (left)

They might have been nose-to-tail in Manhattan, but this was once the closest Honolulu came to traffic congestion. Mule-drawn trams offered twelve miles of track in 1889. The system went all-electric in 1903. The picture shows the bicycle, the horse, the carriage, the tramcar and 'on foot'. Slots ready-cut on the telephone poles display the confidence of the telephone company.

NOW King Street waikiki from Fort

Mighty bastions of business now loom at this intersection, the oldest the 1903 Alexander Young building (left of center), the newest the 1968 building-block Bank of Hawaii (right), both buildings at opposite poles of architectural style. King Street has become one of Honolulu's freeway-like traffic 'arteries'.

THEN Washington Place c.1900

This French Colonial-style residence was raised in the 1840's by one of the Boston sea captains who found in Honolulu a home away from home. His son John Dominis married royalty and became governor of O'ahu. The house was subsequently occupied by Queen Liliuokalani (seated), after her deposition.

NOW Washington Place
Some of the impact of the elegant two-tier lanai was lost with the addition of a porte-cochere (left) and the large 1954 reception lanai (right) as part of extensive renovations. Hawaii's governors have occupied the mansion since 1922.

THEN **Black Point 1920**
The world's most expensive waterfront areas usually start out scenic, balmy and secluded. At right, the clouds over Maui. Remnants of Hawaii's huge sandalwood stand were noted on the foreground slopes by botanists of the 1920's.

NOW **Black Point**
And such areas have a way of staying scenic, balmy and secluded. At center with the classical colonnade is the 1930's Moorish villa built for about $500,000 by heiress Doris Duke.

THEN Union Street mauka 1870

At left is the hip-roofed, dormer-windowed convent of Our Lady Of Peace. Right of center is the hose drying tower of Honolulu fire station built in this year, abandoned in 1893. Dovecotes (lower center) were an attractive downtown feature. Miss Clifton Bartlett no doubt starred at Honolulu music hall.

NOW Union Street mauka

The tower of another public service now dominates the scene, the concrete-framed Hawaiian telephone company building.

THEN Royal Hawaiian Hotel 1931
An economic crash did not affect the steamship set who visited the swank new Spanish-style Royal Hawaiian hotel in chauffeur-driven limousines.

NOW Royal Hawaiian hotel
Today's visitor is more likely to be one of a party on a package tour and rent a bargain bug, somewhat dwarfed by the Royal Hawaiian's Cadillac-sized porte cochere.

THEN King Street at Mililani ewa mauka 1889

Hawaiian tramways started in 1888, the first mass transit, the touchstone of urban lifestyle: a horizontal elevator. At left is Aliiolani Hale, the government office building developed from designs for a royal palace. At right is Honolulu music hall, gutted by fire in 1895 and reopened as the more dignified Opera House, befitting its Italianate design.

NOW **King Street at Mililani ewa mauka** (above)
Marginally profitable public transport has long since been taken over by government. O'ahu's The Bus is one of the few public bus systems widely used by tourists (for a 25-cent round island trip). The Aliiolani Hale became the judiciary building in 1893 and so functions today. The Opera House was pulled down in 1914 and replaced in 1926 by the Spanish Colonial Revival federal building.

THEN Waimea Bay north east panorama 1910

The valleys behind Waimea Bay once held a dense Hawaiian population who certainly made full use of this coral-free body-surfing beach. At right foreground is the Dillingham railway, scrapped after World War II.

NOW **Waimea Bay north east panorama**
The village of Waimea has replaced the coastal smallholdings. For 20 years the tower served as a stone-crushing plant, then was converted into the tower of the village church. Sand hauled from the beach went into concrete. No hotels loom yet over Waimea Bay, although visitors stream daily into the historic valley.

THEN **Fort Street at Chaplain Lane mauka 1870** (left)
   This section of Fort Street was dignified by the Catholic cathedral and convent (right) and medical offices (left), all in the tranquil shade of trees.

NOW **Fort Street at Chaplain Lane mauka**
   The Fort Street mall now serves largely as an adjunct to Honolulu's downtown office district and is as peaceful by 6 p.m. as it was a century ago.

THEN Iolani Palace 1885

The palace was started in 1878 for King Kalakaua, on earnings from the trade agreement he had negotiated in Washington a few years earlier. Built in a mixture of Italian Renaissance and Second Empire styles, it resembled the ornate mansions Kalakaua had seen being built by captains of industry in the eastern U.S.A. The king had private quarters in the pink stucco bungalow behind the palace.

NOW Iolani Palace

After they siezed power in 1893 Hawaii's puritan businessmen named the palace the executive building. They erased the memory of royal decadence so thoroughly that the building almost rotted beyond repair before the state and private donors invested $6 million in restoration. Such was the vengeance of Honolulu's puritans that many Americans were surprised to learn of the palace's existence when it re-opened exactly a century later.

118

THEN Mission Lane 1890
The mission school house, the oldest educational building in Hawaii, exhibits some experimentation by Hiram Bingham's Boston brethren. They originally imported their New England colonial building style, with resultant discomfort, but in the 1835 school house they introduced adobe walls and arched window recesses, recalling the Spanish Colonial style.

NOW Mission Lane (right)
Built on church property, the school house survives, still used as a kindergarten.

119

THEN Honolulu view from Tantalus 1890
Old O'ahu's valleys were either sparsely vegetated with indigenous trees and shrubs or stripped of them by men for profit or by introduced livestock. Here the cultivation of a smallholding contrasts with the bare valley slopes. In the distance Honolulu is all masts.

NOW Honolulu view from Tantalus

Tree planting by Hawaii's department of land and natural resources has transformed this valley into a lush forest reserve composed of dozens of different trees. The 1890 view is blocked by foliage. This higher view is from atop a tree over a cliff; not a tourist viewpoint. In the distance Honolulu is all towers, echoing the masts of old.

THEN Kaahumanu Street at Merchant makai 1890
At left is the 1878 Romanesque-style Bishop Bank, for forty years premises of one of Hawaii's founding mercantile fortunes. At right is the 1854 coral-block Melchers Building, Honolulu's oldest commercial structure. Kaahumanu Street led down to the warehouse of a waterfront shipping merchant.

123

NOW Kaahumanu Street at Merchant makai
Since 1925 the old bank has been rented out for offices and it is now sealed up and refrigerated. The Melchers building, most of its windows blocked in, is used for city offices, and the area between Merchant and Ala Moana boulevard was demolished to make way for a parking garage.

THEN **Kalakaua Avenue at Kalamoku waikiki 1895**
   The trip to the Sans Souci hotel at the foot of Diamond Head along Kalakaua Avenue was long and sedate by mule-drawn tram through farming country. Property bordering Waikiki Beach (right) was fenced off.